Voodoo City Street Spy 2 The Camp

a play, a text and a durational performance by Stan's Cafe

ISBN 978-1-913185-14-5

Published by Stan's Cafe
Birmingham, UK
2020

www.stanscafe.co.uk

Voodoo City © Stan's Cafe 1995
Promotional Photos © Mark Taylor 1995
Production Photos © Anupam Singh 1995
Street Spy 2 © Stan's Cafe 2015
The Camp © Stan's Cafe 2017
Photos © Ben Osborn 2017
Publication © Stan's Cafe 2020

Contents:

Voodoo City	1
Bonus Material	
Production Credits	16
Love Us Or Hate Us, Don't Just Like Us	18
Street Spy 2	22
The Camp	25
The Camp: Getting Cold Feet	28
The Camp Manual	35

Voodoo City

The set is a raised stage covered in roofing felt, surrounded by a scaffolding frame, halogen floods are mounted on the scaffolding. The set is sometimes a roof top and sometimes just resting on the floor.

Opening
Lights up. Performers walk onto stage and climb onto the set almost as if it were a boxing ring. They carry cardboard boxes containing their props, a practice amp and a microphone.

A large old television, mounted on the upstage edge of the set is switched on by Sarah and rubbed until it warms up and a picture of an old time T.V. Star appears.

Life ebbs from the T.V. Star slowly through the course of the performance. This role is played by each performer in turn, each wearing the same spangly suit, slicked back hair and moustache.

Performers settle down to sitting on the scaffolding, the practice amp is hooked onto the set. Everyone is ready.

The Spell
Delivered sat down at pace from up stage, everyone still

Amanda: And this city renounces sleep for fear of its dreams. This city renounces its right to rest for fear of falling apart.
This city renounces sleep and rest and giving of room for thoughts, for fear or chance of streets and devils turning in on themselves.
And we renounce it all, our right to darkness, sleep or rest, or hope, or giving room to thoughts, or anything that might be seen as old or gone or spent or dust, for chance that thoughts turn in and spiralling from the city that spewed us up, than that its turning thoughts left un-propelled by whirlwind

city turning and flying trains, gliding past, covered by the kill cat rattle of drop dead lorry, driven round this big city, big city, big place, lost place and homesick land.
And this is how we make this spell and spell this spell and this is how we raise the sleeping dead of suburb land.

Wild West flies east this Summer, calls up all her powers and fills this sky with vapour trails and sweeps us off her lap.
Wild West fly east and speak in tongues to vodka dreamers, dreaming dreams of telling tales of faking, falling, losing and waiting to count losses.
Wild Wild West we hitch this Skoda to the pick-up van and take it round this Jericho road a thousand times, till we shake the thing apart and spark its axles off the road and wear two grooves around this invalid place. And so we scrape it round and round till we shake the thing to bits and drag this lump of metal round this ring road chaos mayhem place. We drive it, drive it, never can drive it too far, no too far to drive it to.

We conjure, conjuring, playing up a gutter dance, jay-walk, flood-drain and dead litter dance. A stagger wheeling and flinging arms crashing down intoxi-dance.

We dance the timid strangers off this street, we dance the dance for comfort weeks, we dance the coin-op loafers home, we dance this spaced out, save space, jeering lack of hope, grey week-end voodoo, lucky number dance and fuck you, fuck you, we break ourselves on this concrete place.

Tattoo "ready to die" across my face.
Tattoo "kill me now" across my face.
Tattoo your face to fuck.

Make it all clear from here.
Make your statement loud.
Break yourself on this concrete place.

And here we renounce all right to silence,
and all the thoughts that silence brings,
and half the songs we used to sing and all shit we
used to say and half-baked no-hope wishes we
used to wish and quick back handed spliffs of hope
we used to smoke and lost laser check-out maths
we used to do, with nothing much and something
for something, some long-lost something, essence
of something, essence of nothing, before this time,
this charming time, dropped glove, dropped
hanky, hair-grip, foot-fall, watching for a piece of
you time and these charmed, charming charms,
that hold a chunk of you time.

And here we are, we're making charms, to steel us
back from this safe-jar, thermos flask and styro cup
lost limbo. While buildings flicker and witches sit in
burning street corner sofa land, we're making
charms, while pub darts voodoo, back stabbing
politics and pain and pool-hall sex that never was,
is heard abroad, we're pouring whisky on dead
electrics, we're sparking life with burning brandy,
we're making charms and beating beat-up, scratch
kick van, in this distraught destruction place. We're
playing this game of games, telling tales of telling
and telling tales to tell the truth, to out the truth
with no sign of shame. We're playing and crossing
six lanes of traffic with our eyes closed.

We're making charms, we're smashing glass, we're
getting drunk, we're dancing under bridges. We're
playing games of wild chance and living in this city.
We're spilling blood, we're screaming "out", we
send ourselves by phone and haunt this place
while we're still alive.

And "eat dead hope" and "junk this news of
nothing not and no news never".
And "turn this sound up, turn this sound up".
We're blazing up a one way down street and dance
on a taxis' roofs,
find lost chancers Kwik Save charms, black cider
bottled spirits.
We control this city. We control the world.
We're blind guessing, guessing and random dial
punching, guessing, guess punching to speak to
someone, anyone or someone,
punching numbers of anything, any old numbers,
punching and punching and break this, break this,
smash the... smashing and the losing and falling
and the... lost longing,
lost longing loss and the "break this bastard"
and the... she's jumped, jumping, jumped.
Night, sky, light and heartbeat, movement, sensor,
tripping, falling and the
"she's given up, with the dream gods watching and
a child in her arms".
We feather this pavement with jewels
and she breaks herself on this concrete place.

Tune this frequency slowly, tuning through this
dead place, night place, sodium lit and
underground graffiti palace of cabalistic signs.
Through, taboo place, our don't walk here, don't
cross, don't touch, danger electrical conductive
cortex dance and charred place. Through soggy
card and board windowed place, through poisoned
rain and sky, we tune this frequency to you.

From here we can see nowhere, miles of nowhere,
and where are you in here?
Damned you, charmed you,
big city, big city, big smoke and die-punch deity
you.
We renounce different and make ourselves this

place,
spread ourselves over this place,
we are this piss stained place,
and all is us and us, you and you and we are it,
this piss stained place,
and nothing is different from us
and nothing less than us
and no different, no real,
then no real really needs us here
and never should be born.
and take me to a high up angel place,
and hold me to your chest,
and fall with me,
fall with me before I know the difference,
know of not me,
know of other,
all other,
not me,
and out of no control and fit only for crying.

And hold me close as we pass the dream gods
dreaming,
hold me close,
so when you break yourself on this concrete place,
I break myself on you.

And this is why we call you here, from wherever the
hell you're from,
and this is why we call across the skies and call you
to this place.
And all we want, or all we hope to ask of you, is
that simple sums make sense,
that now means now and yes means yes and is
sometimes said to us,
and that there's no more lost, losing, lost and
waiting for the never time,
no more, fuck you, fuck you, we never wanted
anything anyway anytime or how,
no sick guy, cheap tart, left luggage, corn plaster

pool, fake out drug, sick bully-ground less than joke, no out down, never mind, good sense, no way or not a chance and this is why we're freak freaking out, out here.

'coz it's desperation clause and thunder time,
it's pylon climbing prozac bride and shored-up timber scaffold, it's signal breaking, hold the telly, earth yourself to Channel Nine,
and dying stars, blasted, blotted on the ink run sky city night light and shooting stars. She left home at fifteen and wished she'd gone, denim light and sodomised.
And a hundred hundred thousand guesses never get it right, no right to get, get, getting, getting it, no right to get.

We've lashed ourselves to lightning rods, licked our fingers and held them to the sky, "come on sucker strike us down and suicide this place". We were bred for nothing, left to rot, revolting and disorganised, so burn us up, burn us up, burn us, burn us, burn us up. We renounce and scream and spit and dance upon our bodies, in fear of them, all they are and us. And dream us and dream us and dream us and dream us up, with some kind of affection and come to this genius plagued land of devil us and Disney homicidal death of scrounger idle pig, insect-o-cutor genocidal lust of raining desert sand and picking pick, pick, pick-up van and prick, prick, pricking up. You cheap ride, cheap laugh, cheap fucking thrill and big city fusion logic and waste meat gutter, burning drain waste, grim gone other and gone and gone and gone and gone and give us rest, that's not giving up and give us peace, that's not our long gone silence and make us, make, making, make us invent a heaven place with matchboxes, dog ends and old tin cans. And we break your face on this concrete place, to

teach you what real pain is.
And fuck you, fuck you, we never want to die.
And please hold us close to the dream gods
dreaming dreams that make good sense.
And a world that can now be changed, by wishing
on a stick.

The Dance 1

Almost immediately the spell finishes a deep cello opening note is obliterated by city noise cranked up to white noise level. Three of the performers break into a wild freestyle dance about being on the roof top and dancing in your bedroom alone. Sarah joins in later with a slow version of 'The Locomotion', facing out over the city.

Ray shouts down at the street using the practice amp and mic.

Ray: Fuck you, yes you, fuck you. Fuck off!

Graeme on mic through amp over city noise.

Graeme: Heading east, last seen carrying an empty plastic bag, if you are heading west please call us, call 6382149. Call 372 3280. Last seen in a long brown coat, seen outside the post office and heading south. Please call if you recognise this description, call 382 3821 or 741 8901, please call. Call us on 419 8933 or 819 8921 or 814 2381. If you have mysterious eyes or strong opinions please call in confidence on 215 3285.

If you saw a young woman heading west from the bus station with dark hair and white trainers or a man with a small black dog calling out to passers-by, please call.

The weather is set fair and the traffic is beginning to build up. If you're out there call 994 4023 or 820

Possession
Hard into the next scene. On a chair sits Amanda, her arms are obviously those of Sarah whose lap she is sitting on. Ray plays a straight-man to Amanda's 'possessed' woman.

Improvised dialogue and action follow. This starts as a polite conversation, looking out over the city. Amanda has to find excuses for the increasingly embarrassing actions of her out of control hands. The scene pivots around a moment where Ray produces matches and Amanda is in increasing danger of injuring 'herself'; in this way a comedy device turns menacing, matches are lit and Amanda asks for help whilst pulling her own hair and hiding the matches up her jumper. Eventually, from behind, Ray grabs 'Amanda's hands', the matches are dropped and arms relax into her lap. In effect there is a double embrace with both Sarah and Ray's arms around Amanda.

Graeme sits with his legs over the front railing, Ray joins him. Music starts. Graeme takes sample of bits of Ray, a stray hair from the shoulder, a tuft clipped from the fringe, ear wax gathered on a cotton bud, skin from the palm of his hand, dirt from under his nails, all these samples are gathered in a glass jar. The final contribution is spittle. The scene treads an ambiguous line between affection, eroticism and sinister intent.

Ray's samples jar is secured on top of the television with tape and Amanda, who has been sitting possessed in the background, improvises an intense possession moment muttering this spell fragment:

Amanda: We're making charms, we're smashing glass, we're getting drunk, we're dancing under bridges. We're playing games of wild chance and living in this city. We're spilling blood, we're screaming "out", we send ourselves by phone and haunt this place while we're still alive.

And "eat dead hope" and "junk this news of nothing not and no news never".
and "turn this sound up, turn this sound up".
We're blazing up a one way down street, and dance on a taxi's roofs, find lost chancers Kwik Save charms, black cider bottled spirits.

We control this city, we control the world.
We're blind guessing, guessing and random dial punching guessing, guess punching to speak to someone, anyone or someone, punching numbers of anything, any old numbers, punching and punching and break this; break this, smash the... smashing and the losing and falling and the... lost longing, lost longing loss and the "break this bastard".

The scene ends when the 'self-punishment' of hair pulling and stomach punching gets too much and Amanda leaps up protesting momentarily against Sarah's violence.

Terry and June
Immediately preparations begin for a suburban seance scene involving Sarah and Graeme. Ray and Amanda look on laughing and occasionally offering suggestions and encouragement.
The preparations are subdued and involve the orientation of

various household appliances in relation to each other and in reference to some vague history of what's worked in the past.

The seance begins in ludicrous fashion. Graeme pretending to get possessed, then Sarah pretending more convincingly much to Graeme's annoyance. Crazy, cheap, slapstick gags top each other relentlessly with a fake hot chair, soda siphon squirting, a hot iron possessed by a poltergeist and a cheese grater grating hands at random. The 'arms-through' trick from earlier reappears camped right up. Somewhere in the middle is a snatch of crazy sitcom style music.

Sarah, having strangled Graeme, breaks out of the scene and stands at the front of the stage. Graeme embraces her.

Debris from the seance is picked over by Amanda and, with Ray's consent, 'charged' objects are taped to the top of the television, others are put in boxes with the rest thrown off set.

Images
A series of 'filmic' moments follow. Low blue light shows the creation and dismantling of each image, bright halogen floods light the moments. Music continues through the sequence.

Sarah and Graeme embracing on a roof top.

Ray beckoning Amanda along a ledge to safety and holding her close.

Graeme hanging from a scaffolding bar but falling in slow-motion through space.

Sarah making a baby from a jumper and climbing to a window sill, looking down onto the set.

Ray dangles one handed from a scaffold bar.

Amanda falling backwards through a window.

Ray clinging onto a hand, loosing his grip. The hand disappears.
Sarah lies down making a dead body, Amanda and Ray look on.

Graeme's hands appears over the building's edge, he pulls himself up, moves past the death scene and looks down over the building's edge.

Night Sky Light
Graeme is joined by Amanda, they have the microphone between them as they lie on their stomachs look looking down from the roof over the city. Ray has control of the amp, he does the finger movements from the locomotion. Graeme and

Amanda set up a rhythm, reciting their text so it goes in and out of phase

Amanda: Night, sky, light, heartbeat, movement, sensor, tripping.
Graeme: Night, sky, light, and heartbeat, movement, sensor, tripping.

They complete two complete circles of coming in and out of phase, adding two extra "heartbeats" to the second repetition of the third circle and six extra to the sixth and fifth respectively then coming into phase and ending:

Both: Falling and the, she's jumped, jumping, jumped.

Sarah has been lip-synching the sequence, taking alternative words from each speaker, she synchs the whole of the final phrase. After the text Ray sets feed-back screaming through the microphone, Sarah holds a cassette player blasting out voodoo dance crazy music to the microphone which is shortly drowned out by the same music at extreme volume through the venue speakers.

The Dance 2
There is an extended freestyle dance sequence, with people throwing themselves to the edge of the roof, getting very dizzy, freaking out. Self-obsessed, Ray is craziest of all and jumps from the building, shocked to find himself landing on the floor he watches the others dance themselves into a dazed and exhausted state whilst he sips at a Pepsi Max.

With the music finished and feedback still howling through the practice amp Amanda, Sarah and Graeme flake out, staring out and hallucinating. Ray switches off the amp.

The T.V. Star rallies himself just enough to produce a microphone (the same one used by the cast) and sing a number of repetitions of:

TV Star: Hold me close, hold me close as we pass the dream gods dreaming.

The television flickers as the TV Star's chin slumps to his chest.

Building the City
Music starts as a model city is constructed. Old railway tickets form roads, match boxes, books, cereal boxes, small paint pots, marker pens, the cheese grater, a set of scales, a dish rack make buildings, a couple of lengths of carpet create hills and some fairy lights finish the scene off.

Ray watches.

Ray: We've lashed ourselves to lightning rods, licked our fingers and held them to the sky, "come on sucker, strike us down and suicide this place". We renounce and scream and spit and dance upon our bodies, in fear of them, all they are and us, and dream us and dream us and dream us and dream us up, with some kind of affection and come to this genius plagued land of devil us and give us rest that's not giving up and give us peace, that's not our long gone silence and make us, make, making, make us invent a heaven place with matchboxes, dog ends and old tin cans.

With lighting cross fading, a plant mister making rain, a couple of matchbox cars added and an aeroplane flying over head the junk suddenly looks like a city.

The music ends. Ray is the only person lit, he starts the final text but his voice is replaced as he lip-synchs the rest of the cast. For the last four words his mouth is closed.

A, G & S: And we break your face on this concrete place to teach you what real pain is
and fuck you, fuck you, we never want to die.
and please hold us close to the dream gods

dreaming dreams that make good sense.
and a world that can now be changed, by wishing on a stick.

Blackout.

Voodoo City Production Credits

Devised and performed by
Sarah Dawson
Amanda Hadingue
Ray Newe
Graeme Rose

Direction and Text
James Yarker

Original Music
Richard Chew with Jon Ward

Lighting
Paul Arvidson

Set and Costume
Stan's Cafe

Promotional Photographs
Mark Taylor

Performance Photographs
Anupam Singh

Graphic Design
Simon Ford

The piece was premiered at mac Birmingham
15th 16th 17th February, 1995

Commissioned by mac and mac New Works Trust
with Funding from West Midlands Arts
and Birmingham City Council

Love us or hate us don't ever just like us

Voodoo City (1995) was made in Stan's Cafe's 'teenage years' when the company was thrashing around trying to work out who it was, where it belonged and what made it it.

The 'real world' is a scary and bewildering place for a new born theatre company and so initially we were relieved to discover that everyone seemed to quite like us. As toddlers we had rapidly ticked off our initial goals, we could walk and talk and wipe our own bums. *Bingo In The House Of Babel* (1994) had been made with proper Arts Council England money so now we were in big school and ripe to be bullied, unless we shaped up quickly. We needed to assert ourselves and set some new targets.

We knew that ambition for Stan's Cafe should never be about survival, being fashionable or earning riches, it should be about being vital. I wanted Stan's Cafe to be a company that people felt passionately about. We needed to be loved, not by everyone, that would be unrealistic, but some people and if the price of being loved by some, meant being hated by others, so be it. We'd rather be a company over which fist fights were fought than one which elicited universal polite applause. Our new mantra should be 'Love us or hate us, don't ever just like us'.

It was a simple goal to set but difficult to know what it meant in practice. Our interpretation was that whatever we made next had to be more extreme than anything we had ever made before.

Voodoo City was an uncomfortable show to make, I suspect we were all mostly unhappy throughout. I was keen to make a show that was 'one thing' rather than a number of themed rehearsal room ideas arranged in an order with their edges blurred to give them the illusion of unity, but I had no idea how to do this. Ironically, the privilege of funding meant we had to pay people properly and could only afford four weeks devising time, so the pressure was intense. Graeme Rose, the company's co-founder, was returning to join the team that had devised *Bingo In The House Of Babel* and when there were artistic differences it was difficult for everyone to work out whose opinions should have what weighting. Personally things were getting very intense, Stan's Cafe had become the sole focus of my life and I was seeing signs of madness on the streets:

Things I have seen

There's a house with huge black metal plates screwed down over all the windows and a metal door that's been welded closed and I cross the road before then.

And there's a street corner, where sometimes you find a huge pile of soggy white bread, a really big pile, and it's there for a few days before someone must take it away and I try to avoid that.

And sometimes I see this old woman with a shopping trolley and her face powdered totally white and a green dye in her hair and it's as if she's never there because no-one ever sees her.

And there's the woman who shouts at the vegetables outside Spar, just picks them up shouting and puts them down again.

And there are burnt-out cars on the street and a three legged dog.

And the road has been marked up with crosses and numbers but never dug up.

And there's a van with newspaper taped inside all the windows all the way round, for no reason.

And one day I noticed how many children's shoes
and gloves there are lying in the gutters
There where two black cider bottles laid parallel
on the pavement
A dead cat spread belly up with its mouth open
And on all the street corners there are foam sofas,
which I never sit on.

Every Sunday in the City Centre you find blood on
the pavements
and phone boxes ring with no one to answer
them
and water sometimes just bubbles up through the
pavement.

And there was a old guy who said he was a
shaman and would bless me for a quid
and there was an old man banging a biscuit tin lid
with a stick, just standing by the road banging this
lid with a stick, banging away,
and I gave them both some money, just in case.

And I saw lightning strike this tower block twice,
so I came up here.

James Yarker 1995

On reflection maybe *Voodoo City*, with all its references to ritual acts, was itself Stan's Cafe's rite of passage. Our next show *Ocean of Storms* (1996) felt like a new more mature, controlled and self-confident 'us', more 'one thing', extreme but in a more sophisticated way, the company was finding its own voice and identity. I suspect without this jolt of voodoo magic we would never have made this transition to adulthood.

Street Spy 2

In 2015 we were asked by a 'retail organisation' to contribute to a publication they were planning linking them with the art scene in Birmingham. We wrote them our second *Street Spy* challenge. They had editorial control and wanted us to change some things we didn't want changed, so it was never published, until now.

Today, on the streets of Birmingham test your observational skills. Don't let any aspect of the city pass you by. Prove yourself a Street Spy. Read this list then go out hunting for everything on it. Tick off what you find then check your score to see what level of Street Spy you are.

Yellow paper bag	1
Floral print	1
Sunglasses as headband	1
Special offer	1
Smiling face	1
Child with balloon	2
Three young women arm in arm	3
Child on Dad's shoulders	2
Two men holding hands	3
Man with beard	1
Man with beard but no moustache	5
Man with moustache but no beard	3
Clean shaven man	0
Odd socks	5
Tattooed neck	3
Sunburn	4
Numbers on pavement	5
Two people carrying one bag between them	5
One person carrying five bags	3
One person carrying more than five bags	4
High heels (running)	5
Suitcase (being pulled)	3

Shoelaces (that need tying)	5
Guitar (over shoulder)	7
Skateboard	3
Folding bike	5
Unicycle	30
Cobbled street	10
Snooker hall	10
Proofing house	30
Raindrops in puddles	5
Silver coin on the ground	10
Memorial	5
Flowers taped to a lamppost	10
Busker	5
Two magpies	10
A single police officer	10
Bus queue	3
Car you wish you drove	3
Car with top down	6
Kid with hood up	1
WAIT	1
STOP	1
GIVE WAY	1
NO BALL GAMES	10
Red man	1
Shamrock	5
Giant green man	20
Someone drinking beer	5
People laughing	10
Discarded can	5
Your own discarded can	-5
CCTV Camera	3
Broken Glass	2
Wires over head	3
Helicopter	10
Niqab	5
Belly button	5

Branded pants riding up above jeans	2
Crucifix	3
Evangelist	5
Neon	5
Rainbow	20
Pillar of Light	1000
Fight	-50
Car crash	-100
Volcano spewing fire	1000
Angelic Host singing	1000
Sheep	20
Goats	40
A familiar face in the crowd	10
Charred remains	5
Somewhere something once was	5
Somewhere something will soon be	5
A dandelion	20
Earth	5
Your own hands out in front of you, empty hands, palms to the sky, relaxed, feeling the air while you slowly count to ten	20
The Earth	20
Birmingham, today, tonight, as it is	100

Results

Less than 100 — You are a Kerb Crawler, a low eye leveller, lift it before you lose it.

100 – 1000 — You are a City Dweller, a traffic dodger, hunt smarter to shine brighter.

More than 1000 — You are a true Street Spy, a poet of the pavement, make something good happen.

The Camp

For *The Camp*, Stan's Cafe are spending 48 hours in two Iron Age forts at Earls Hill, Pontesford, as travellers from a time far in the future. They will be living a minimal existence, without current technology. Depending when they arrive visitors may be invited to share food or drink in the camp, find firewood, hold the camp's flag, join in a simple game or just to sit and talk. All the time the true stars of the show will be around us; the views, the sun and moon, clouds, rocks, trees, fresh air and grass under foot.

Original promotional text.

The Camp: Credits

Performed by
Graeme Rose, Craig Stephens, Amy Ann Haigh
and James Yarker

Costumes by
Denise Stanton and Kay Wilton

Photographs by Ben Osborn
Lower camp hut by Yinka Danmole
Project management by Laura Killeen
Executive producer Roisin Caffrey

Commissioned by the National Trust
as part of the Heartland project
in partnership with:
Arts Alive,
Shropshire Hills AONB Partnership
and
Stiperstones & Corndon Hill
Country Landscape Partnership.

Stan's Cafe Theatre would like to thank all the commissioners for their inspirational idea, faith in us and support. We would also like to thank: the Friends of Pontesford Hill, Ben Osborn, Ruth Gibson and Mary Keith.

"This commission asked artists to find ways of encouraging visitors to come and enjoy Shropshire's spectacular landscape; The Camp is our response.

It is an excuse to spend some time in this amazing place and maybe reflect on the lives we currently lead. We hope you enjoy your time with us."

James Yarker – Artistic Director, July 2017

The Camp: Getting Cold Feet

For years we would set out Stan's Cafe's mission statement by describing Elizabethan explorers sailing off into the unknown, mapping new territory, bringing back treasures and taking audiences to see new sights. Now, almost twenty years later, we finally have a project that can live up to this metaphor and perhaps take the edge off its pretension.

The Camp is a rare example of Stan's Cafe making a pure site specific performance. Our commissioning brief was to make a performance to showcase the spectacular wonders of the Shropshire Hills and our proposal, to establish and live in a futuristic/ancient campsite for 48 hours, was inspired by the Iron Age hill forts we saw in that landscape. Once accepted this idea was then shaped by the character and specific challenges of the chosen performance site on Earls Hill where the never to be repeated performance took place.

Because there was no shared audience experience, no script, no video and few photographs, this essay acts as map of that place and a record of that time. Because performing the piece was an intensely personal as well as collective experience what follows is a mix of my perspective with that of Amy, **Craig** and Graeme.

I approached the performance with an acute, fearful sense of foreboding.

The Camp couldn't be rehearsed it could only be prepared for, like an expedition. We didn't know who we would meet or how they would react to us, we could only agree strategies for their engagement. We didn't know when we would be alone and for how long, but knew we needed to know why we were there, so we tested ourselves with questions, backstories and logical tests. We wanted to be prepared for all eventualities.

Brain scanning to identify where our vulnerabilities might lie; physical vulnerabilities, creative vulnerabilities. We would be wild in uncharted territory, trusting our instinct, our wisdom, our wherewithal, our stamina. Working alongside, or working in spite of Nature? Wet weather provision topmost on my list of concerns

Several days on. The memory lingers intensely, and is hard to shake off. **It was an experience to share but also to savour alone.**

The performance started on Friday night with weather as brutal as late July can offer. It rained a fair bit on a mixed Saturday as well. Extended respite came on a lovely Sunday. We had a modest stream of visitors, some visiting us intentionally, some meeting us accidentally. On both nights more than a dozen people stayed overnight with us sleeping out and eating round an open fire.

We took off our watches and abandoned our phones. Leaving the world of phone-signals, watches and clocks, to commune with each other and the landscape felt vital. *Time no longer seemed important, we were no longer controlled by it.* **The Camp felt like a moment out of time.** *There was no urgency. We ate when hungry and slept when tired.* I saw countless images aching to be photographed, but this way of thinking had to be abandoned, we were living for here and now, the next meal and the coming night. We were present, standing on the earth as it turned.

I thought about the people who had lived here thousands of years ago. I admired their resilience. *I thought a lot about the homeless having to continuously endure the elements. It made me thankful.*

We have each adopted a tarpaulin in lieu of a waterproof costume, I'm sitting out the rain on a log thinking of Tehching Hsieh, I can't believe we've been so over optimistic about the weather, my thesis is proven; we're pathetic.

Damp grass, damp groundsheet. Water dropping from the skies, dripping from trees; water climbing upwards through absorbent materials.

I think that footwear will make or break us. I'm feeling grateful for the small things; the comfort of well-fitting boots, the comfort of a damp sock that is at least warm.

I choose these shoes as they are the most rudimentary I could find and as a consequence I'm now thinking of trench foot and Vietnam War films of the 1980s, the phrase 'getting cold feet' is no longer merely a figure of speech, my enthusiasm is low and I marvel at how sensible Amy, Craig and Graeme are to be properly shod. **I was glad to be with the people I was with.**

We felt the hard work necessary simply to stay warm and fed. Firewood was abundant, everywhere and I was amazed that it lit so easily, given the wood's dampness and the rottenness of so much of it.

A thick rotten stick starts to steam and then, from its jagged broken ends, a host of minuscule ants emerge, frantically climbing up away from the flames; their world has taken a turn for the worse, abruptly unfathomably and catastrophically. We look down on their lives from beyond the fire.

We concoct stews from random collections of vegetables and find it delicious and nutritious. We have vegetable stew for every meal except breakfasts, when we have porridge. I was perfectly happy with our diet, though every stew we ate would have been improved by the inclusion of more potato. I recognise that potato remains my favourite vegetable. I don't care about the grubbiness of our tools, or our hands; I don't care about the rainwater in our pot, the green-wood smoke infusing our every mouthful, our clothing, our breath.

I'd been thinking of the Anthropocene; and here was the opportunity to contemplate it on a (plastic) plate - to consider how much our lives have left the earth, how much the urban mindset conveniently forgets the means of production from which food and fuel, and yes, culture, emerge.

Quail eggs prove a surprising hit - even the most worldly wise visitors appeared never to have tasted them before. I maintain an insistence they are tiny chicken eggs from tiny chickens; no one was fooled - at least not for long. It's all a facade; the water is from a tap barely 500m away but the food is hardly local sourced and 'bee juice' is from a German discount store with a scrap of honeycomb added to give it a faux foraged feel. We're doing our best, we're drinking mint tea from mint leaves.

We share our food with visitors and in turn they share rare treats with us. **We experienced the kindness of strangers in simple transactions:** a thin slice of cake, a hunk of homemade bread, a lump of 'sugar bean mud'. We have toothbrushes to trade, we seek a new 'fire starter'.

Interactions with visitors were enjoyable. Most were accepting of our fiction and interacted in a playful and inquisitive way. Conversation flowed from fiction to reality seamlessly. The two worlds merged.

Our personal fictions can be difficult to sustain; awkward or disingenuous, too liable to slip onto the wrong side of the sharpened blade of pretence. The rules of engagement require some to and fro and must be recalibrated on each separate encounter. I struggle with some and the fiction evaporates. Talking with the Wildlife Trust and Friends of Pontesford Hill, knowledgeable locals, I wish I'd been better prepared with knowledge of tree identification. Our evening's guests dwell on the actual not fictional.

We'd imagined that the glow of the evening campfire would be ideal for the rolling improvised twisted historical storytelling technique we had been rehearsing but strangely, people seemed to be enjoying the here and now too much for us to launch into our deception. **The Camp invented itself as it went along, changing its parameters according to the visitors.** Openness and honesty are the tools which lubricate this community. **We met some lovely people and were privileged to hear their stories of travel and adventure.** We listening to their stories; it feels a privilege to be in their company and to share this unlikely moment together with them. They have been waiting for this opportunity, longer perhaps than we have known ourselves. Perhaps we are time travellers and they knew about us long before the idea took shape?

Alone on the hill top, innocent strangers regularly ask "what are you doing here?" I say "waiting for my family," they seem happy with that. We improvise a coy, flirtatious dance back and forth across the line separating truth from fiction. Our preparations serve me well, I am ready with all the answers and some of the questions.

The interactions with children felt particularly special. Our curiosity about the past (their present) allowed them to question the function and necessity of everyday objects. They recognise the broken plastic figure of Shaggy, but how do you explain Scooby-Do, The Mystery Machine and television to people who appear not to know anything useful?

A boy calls to his friend "there's a man up there who knows NOTHING!"

Children teach us the first couple of lines of the Scooby-Do theme song, they misremember it. Just one generation on and the aural history is already mutating. After weeks struggling to work out how to integrate a local musician's songs into *The Camp* it's now clear why poorly remembered TV theme tunes are far more apt for our performance than anything else.

Folk memory founded on redundant contemporary tropes and crap idioms from pop culture is exciting to dwell upon; back into a world of Riddley Walker. Plastic detritus as future treasure. Stan belongs in this world.

Although lacking sleep, I felt surprisingly energised. Being in the fresh air awakened me. **I felt cold, wet, hot, tired, energised, fit, unfit.** Gravity and that hill are our implacable foes. Travelling from the low camp to the high camp was a significant commitment. Carrying bags of sand to the summit I recall the opening shots of *Aguirre, the Wrath of God* and Sebastian Salgado's photographs of gold mining in Brazil and remember with humility that our performance is an act of decadence.

Ludicrous, potentially dangerous, dragging the fire bowl to the summit was a challenge of epic proportions, eclipsing even memories of Canute's Sisyphusian ordeal in Kendal*. Nothing great is easy and this was far from easy. Our success was perhaps the greatest individual triumph of the weekend, an achievement of Fitzcarraldian proportions.

We shared a commitment to going beyond what can reasonably be expected, in order to create, for the audience, something unexpected. Carrying a smaller fire bowl to the summit would have been considerably easier - but what would have been the point? I kept thinking 'it could be worse, we could be building bloody Stonehenge'.

We had to pause the ascent in order to change into our costumes. The final push to the summit would be part of the performance and all the better for that.

Are costumes were of a whiteness that promised to bear the marks of the forest, of the terrain, of the territory. Rope bound material over shoes added an extra degree of difficulty and hazard - no wonder civilisation invented leather and laces, buckles and zips and velcro - why didn't we set this performance in a utopian future of intelligent fabrics and anti-gravity fire bowls?

Holding the flag felt important and imperative. Having to withstand the wind felt empowering.

Regularly, I think how amazing, Amy, Craig and Graeme look in their costumes in this context, especially holding that flag. These are moments from an extraordinary other reality, a massive rainbow, a blistering sunset and an epic wind.

There were moments of sublime beauty as I stood on the hilltop alone with the flag looking out across the countryside in all directions.

The flag acted as a beacon for the local-visitors. They commented that it could be seen for miles and that they'd used it to detect our presence upon traveling to the hill.

This was our presence in a distilled image, validating us.

I could imagine those who had visited still having a connection with us once left as they looked towards the flag.

The incredible Saturday sunset will stay in my mind for many years to come. The 'overnighters' shared this sunset with us. They wouldn't have been there looking that way if it hadn't been for *The Camp*; this is what it's for.

Driving home in the van was something to truly treasure; dirt, exhaustion, warmth and delirious hilarity in the aftermath of our communal adventure. The moments of sublime beauty will prevail, long after the moments of damp, sleepless misery have disappeared from memory.

`It was a hardcore, gentle performance. I wanted to stay I was happy to go.`

* Graeme's reference here is to our valiant but failed attempt to carry gallons of water up a waterlogged hill to Kendal Castle, for a performance of *Canute The King* in 1993.

The Camp Manual

Time Logic
There are places, such as Earl's Hill, where time becomes unmoored and different eras drift close and touch. Here and now 2017 has become entangled with a distant future version of itself and temporarily four people exist in both times at the same time.

Cast
Graeme = Rose   Craig = Ash   Amy = Victory   James = Thin

Activities at Lower Camp
At the lower camp we make charms to help people find the way. We use twine that we found on our travels and sticks and bracken that we pick up on site. The tent/structure has been here a long time, it was built by someone else.

"Some of my family are at the top of the hill. If you could take them this… [water or food] it would be very helpful. They always need more 'dead fall' and 'chat' for the fire [fallen branches and dry sticks], so if ,on your way up, you find any chat lying on the ground they would be very happy for you to take them. If you make a charm you could take it home or add it to the path going up to help people on their way".

At dusk we light the fire at lower camp and we share stories that we've heard.

Activities at Upper Camp
We hold up the flag so people know we're there, visitors are very welcome to help us. We keep the fire going and so need to collect dry wood for this.
We brew tea and cook food. Visitors are welcome to help us with this and to share the food and drink.
We may play games including one that is throwing stones into squares made with sticks and twine.
We talk to people.

Answers to possible questions:
Who are you?
We're people, from a family (family refers to relations, friends and fellow villages).

Where are you from?
Over there (the East – pointing to the tower in Ironbridge). The tower is a rare landmark poking up from a landscape entirely covered by trees. The buildings visible in 2017 are rubble within the forest that we see. We have left a village with a family there; they may come and join us if we find a better place.

What are you doing here?
Waiting for our friends to return. We are looking for somewhere better to live, our friends have gone out to search for our next campsite, we are waiting for them to report back.

Why are you moving?
To find somewhere easier to live, with a better food supply.

What's the flag for?
So people know we're here. So our family can find us again. Whenever it's daylight we need the flag to be visible.

How long are you here for?
Until our family return and we decide where to go next.

What's it all about – who's paying Etc.
I don't know, that person over there is good at answering those kind of questions (point to commissioner or Roisin or Laura).

We are mildly curious about everything and not shocked by anything. We are generally positive but also cautious and a little bit distant.

Photographs
We are happy to have our photographs taken, but we're not exactly sure what they are for. We tend to not look into the lens but above and to one side.

Mobile Phones
We've seen them but never one that works, so never knew that they 'did' anything.

Toothbrushes
We found a big stack in some ruins a long time ago, now they are available to trade. The things we are most interested in are cigarette lighters. We are interested generally in exchange but the lighters are what we want most.

Dogs
We are anxious about dogs as we have no domesticated dogs and wild dogs can be dangerous.

Airplanes
We've never seen them before but if they are pointed out to us then we can see them. We don't know what they are (let's not say "ooh heap big metal bird in sky").

Cows, sheep and other wildlife
We don't mind them but we don't eat them as their meat made our ancestors ill. Milk makes us ill too.

Vocabulary
Down the slider (hill)
Up the rake (hill)
Waterdogs (clouds)
I think it's going to blatter (rain heavily)
It's been gleamy (sunshine and showers)
It's very hasky (dry)
We'll have a cant (story telling)
Dead fall (fallen branches)
Chats (dead sticks)

About the illustration and design

The illustrations for the covers of these books were undertaken by students at Birmingham City University as the final module of their first-year illustration course during the Spring/Summer of 2018. The images were developed through workshops using variations of the theatre-devising methods employed by Stan's Cafe but adapted and applied to the making of visual work. The resulting work was shown in the pop-up exhibition *The Something Of Somebody Something* at Stan's Cafe's venue @AE Harris in May 2018.

The design concept of the books was produced by final year Graphic Design student Aimee Chapman. These were then further developed for print in a collaborative process between Stan's Cafe and the University's Innovation Product Support Service (IPSS) which involved helping the company to select appropriate DTP software, undertaking training and selecting a suitable print on demand service.

Gareth Courage
Lecturer in Illustration
Birmingham City University

www.ingramcontent.com/pod-product-compliance
Lightning Source LLC
Chambersburg PA
CBHW071759080526
44588CB00013B/2301